Zac's Story

Did I cause this ...?

Lynley Barnett

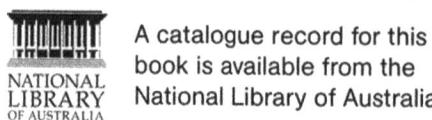
A catalogue record for this book is available from the National Library of Australia

Copyright Text: © 2023: Lynley Barnett
Copyright Illustrations: ©2023 Helen Iles
All rights reserved.
ISBN: 978-1-922727-93-0

Linellen Press
265 Boomerang Road
Oldbury, Western Australia
www.linellenpress.com.au

This is Zac's story.

I am Zac. I am eleven and am still at primary school but I will be in Secondary school next year. The Secondary school is near the primary school, just a little further down the road.

When my mum and dad sat me down to tell me they were getting divorced, I was not surprised. They have been fighting so much I have had to shut myself in my bedroom and put my earphones on.

I have been very upset because they fight so much. My friend Marcus says his house used to be just like mine, but that was when he was little, so we have been sharing our stories. Somehow that seems to help.

I am a School Prefect in my last year in Primary and I have a lot of important things to do. I wish when I came home that the house was peaceful like it used to be.

And they don't realise that it is so hard to do homework when everyone in the house is upset. My older sister won't stay home; she just goes out to her friend's place.

Meal times are awful. Why can't they just try to be friendly during meals?

Everything Dad does is wrong; everything Mum says is wrong. I threw up last week after tea. I felt so sick hearing the angry words they were saying.

I go to my room a lot now because I can shut the door and just not listen to Mum and Dad.

I want to shout "Stop, just stop!" But they don't listen to me much anymore.

I have wondered if they are splitting up because of me. I really don't know what I might have done to make this happen. But could it have been because of me?

I know it costs a lot of money to send me to school and to play sports. Would it help if I quit Junior AFL? I would do that if it would help them. I would even give up Surf Life Saving if that would help too.

This might sound awful but I'm really hoping that I'll come home from school one day and it has all happened. I am so tired. I explained it to my teacher Mrs Burns last week and now she checks up on me every day. At least she listens.

But, before they split up I wish they would sit down with us and ask us what we would like.

I would say:
Please don't make me change schools.
Please don't make me stop playing Junior AFL or going to the beach with the Surf Life Saving Club. These are my friends. I know I said I would give these sports up but I really didn't mean it.

Please just don't change anything at all. I like my routine, I like my friends. I like my school.

I would like to see lots of Dad or Mum if one of them shifts out. I want Dad to come to Footy, and I want to go to the big games with him like always. How would this happen if I had to go between two houses?

Please tell my other teachers as well. It is too embarrassing for me to do this.

And please tell our friends what is happening, and do my grandparents know? Mrs Burns wanted to know if I could go to the School Counsellor.

Can I?

What I don't understand is how all of this will work. Where will I sleep? My head spins from trying to figure out what is going to happen. I really need to know. Please tell me what is going to happen to me.

When Mrs Burns asked me how I felt the other day I told her I am just so confused and angry and sad and mad, and sometimes the lot all together. She laughed a little at this, and then so did I. It did sound all mixed up.

She did tell me though that I am allowed to have a bunch of feelings when parents are splitting up, and when things are bad she suggested I run twice around the playground, so I did. It helped me but I don't really know why.

Right now, Mum is out looking for work, so Marcus's mother collects us both from school and I stay there until Mum picks me up. Marcus's mother is so kind to me. I have cried a few times at her place but Mum and Dad do not know.

Mrs Mac, she calls herself, so that's what we call her too.
She makes a mean hot chocolate on a cold day. And she makes me one when I have been crying. Marcus has a fabulous Leggo set and we build until I forget what I was crying about.

I do love my mum and my dad, and I have tried but I can't make anything better. I just want it all to be over, and then we can be friends again. And when I asked Mrs Mac "Will they ever be friends again?" she said, "Perhaps not like before, but they will be kinder to each other."

I'm not like I was before. I worry a lot, mostly about where I will live, what school I will go to and if I will lose my friends. And it seems none of this has been settled yet. I wish it was.

About the Author

Lynley Barnett spent many years working in Perth WA as an A.D.R.P. (Alternate Dispute Resolution Practitioner) or Mediator to you. She worked thousands of hours in Mediation, with adults, couples, and businesses.

She wrote this book to help children whose parents are divorced or divorcing.

www.ingramcontent.com/pod-product-compliance
Lightning Source LLC
Chambersburg PA
CBHW051350110526
44591CB00025B/2958